Respect

Dare to Care, Share, and Be Fair!

Written by
Ted and Jenny O'Neal

Illustrated by
R. W. Alley

ONE
CARING
PLACE

Abbey Press
St. Meinrad, IN 47577

*For Scott and Jason
and for Gramma O'Neal*

Text © 2001 Ted O'Neal and Jenny O'Neal
Illustrations © 2001 St. Meinrad Archabbey
Published by One Caring Place
Abbey Press
St. Meinrad, Indiana 47577

Library of Congress Catalog Number
2001089652

ISBN 978-0-87029-353-5

Printed in the United States of America

A Message to Parents, Teachers, and Other Caring Adults

Respect is one of those words getting a lot of attention today. You could say it's like the word *water* getting a lot of attention in the middle of the desert: You certainly notice when it's *not* there, and everyone wishes there were more of it!

Especially when it comes to teaching and raising children, we need to pay attention to the virtue of respect. We know that individuals form so many of their attitudes, patterns of behavior, and everyday habits in their youth. We know that childhood is the place for virtues to be taught—or, more accurately, "caught."

We remember the concepts our own parents and teachers tried to impart—politeness, honesty, tolerance, generosity, patience, kindness. While these may not have been the exact words used, these were the inherent values that our parents and teachers tried to instill. The actual words we heard were probably more like: "Wait your turn"; "Do unto others"; "Walk a mile in his shoes"; "Be sure to be there on time."

The best lessons in respect, of course, involved no words at all but were taught through example: Dad offered the first helping of mashed potatoes to Mom. Gramma told Gramps she was sorry to keep him waiting. Mom helped you make lemonade for your friends. Teacher made certain every kid had exactly three seconds at the water fountain!

Is the "old-fashioned" and quaint virtue of respect ready for a comeback in our modern society? We all know it is sorely needed in a world more and more diverse, more and more congested, more and more interdependent. We are in this together, after all.

May the words and pictures in this book help us bring home for our children the value of respect!

—Ted and Jenny O'Neal

What IS Respect?

When you hear the word "respect," you might think of a servant bowing down and paying "respect" to the king in a fairy tale. Respect can mean "bowing down," but it has other meanings, too.

Respect is what is called a "virtue." It's a good way to be—and a way to be good. It's a way to care about others, ourselves, and our world. When we have the virtue of respect, we try to treat people and our whole world with extra love and kindness.

Showing respect might mean standing up and giving an older person your seat, or holding the door for someone. Respect also means being polite, being a good sport, being honest and fair.

The Golden Rule

"The Golden Rule" goes like this: "Do to others as you want others to do to you." That means: Try to treat others the same way you want them to treat you. When you follow the Golden Rule, you show respect. You care about other people's feelings and rights.

For example: If you borrow a friend's video game, you need to take care of it just as if it was your own. When you return it, you say, "Thanks for letting me use this"—just like you would want your friend to do if he borrowed your video game.

Some kids may make fun of you for being nice or polite to others, but you can just ignore them. Following the Golden Rule is caring and cool!

How to Show Respect

You show respect when you play the game your cousin wants to play even if it's not your favorite one. You treat a new classmate with respect by saying hello and talking to him. You are respectful toward your sick neighbor when you give her flowers to show you care.

Respect can also mean showing appreciation. When you say to your friend, "We sure had fun sled-riding!" this is a way of thanking him for being your friend.

Even being ready on time when your friend comes to pick you up is a way of showing respect. You care enough about him that you don't want to keep him waiting.

What NOT to Do

Some things are NOT respectful: teasing, yelling, being rude, not waiting your turn, fighting, leaving your room a mess.

Respect means NOT making fun of the things other people like to do—like when your Dad is watching a boring TV show, or your brother is pretending to be Ken Griffey, Jr.

Sometimes kids do things with friends that they would never do on their own. They might "go along with the crowd" and say mean things about a classmate or throw rocks at a neighbor's car. But respect means doing what's right no matter who you are with.

Different Is GOOD!

If your classmate likes to put ketchup on macaroni, that doesn't mean he deserves to be teased. People are different and like different things. Maybe some things *you* do seem strange to other people!

It's hard to understand how other people can like different things than we do. But *everyone* deserves respect—even people with funny-colored bedrooms, weird hair, or strange clothes.

We can all have different opinions, tastes, and feelings and still get along. In fact, you might even find out that ketchup on macaroni is *good*!

Try to Understand

Respecting other people means trying to understand them—to feel what they feel. One good way to understand someone is to make believe that you are that person.

If Dad cooks something you don't like, pretend that you are a parent, trying to feed your family healthy food. Maybe you are tired after working all day, or in a hurry. How do you feel when someone calls your cooking "yucky"?

If your sister is crabby, try to understand why. Maybe she doesn't feel well, or she had a really hard test at school. Maybe she would even like to talk about it—a little later when she's in a better mood.

Magic Words

There are some magic words that will take you far in the world—and make other people feel good, too. They are words like "Please," "Thank you," "Excuse me," "I'm sorry." Words like "Move!" or "Shut up!" are not magic words. They just upset people.

Many of us are taught to say, "Good morning" and "Good night" to everyone in our family. It's also nice to say, "Hello," when you come home from school or a friend's house. Try to at least say, "I'm home," instead of asking right away, "What's for dinner?"

The words we use have the power to hurt people—or to heal people. Out of respect, we try to use good words instead of bad words.

Pay Attention

Just paying attention to someone is a good way to show respect—especially when you're busy or would rather be doing something else.

Try to listen to your brother, instead of interrupting him. Try to notice when someone looks nice, or does a good job. If you tell your mom, "I like the way your hair looks," it makes both of you feel good.

Practice respecting your teacher. Pay attention instead of talking or doodling in your notebook. Raise your hand instead of yelling out answers.

Animals need respect, too. Pay attention to your pets. Remember to feed them, give them baths, and play with them.

When You're Angry

It's good to share your feelings with people—in a respectful way. That can be hard when you don't agree with them or feel angry. But there are ways to share your feelings and care for others' feelings at the same time.

Instead of saying something like, "How come you bumped into me, Stupid?" you could say, "That really hurt when you bumped into me. Will you please be more careful?"

Respect for the Whole World

Respect means believing that every person on earth has value. It means understanding that the world belongs to all of us and we belong to the world—and we all belong to God.

It's good to learn about people around the world from books or TV. When we learn about the way they live and work and speak, it helps us to see life through their eyes and to have respect for them.

We can show respect for the whole world—even for people not born yet—by taking care of all creation. We can try to pick up litter and to recycle. We can join an environment club at school to learn about respecting the earth.

PUT TRASH HERE

LITTER PATROL

Fairness

Treating others fairly is a big part of respect.

Sometimes people are treated unfairly because they are too old or too young, too big or too little. Sometimes people are treated unfairly because of the color of their skin or what they believe. But everyone deserves respect.

Respect may mean speaking up for people who can't speak up for themselves. It can also mean speaking up for yourself if you're not being treated fairly.

Remember, what you say and do—and what you don't say or do—can help or hurt our world. It's your choice.

Expect Respect

You deserve respect, too! Be nice to yourself. After you do a good deed, such as helping your dad plant flowers, give yourself (and Dad!) a special treat—like ice cream.

Giving respect to others will help you to get respect from them. When you treat other people kindly, you are more likely to be treated kindly in return.

This doesn't always happen, though. Sometimes people just forget to respect. Or they may not have learned yet how to be caring and kind. You can't control what other people say or do, but you *can* control how *you* will act.

Good Habits

Respect is not always fun or easy. It takes time and effort. But it's easier when it becomes a habit. That means you need to practice respect every day.

Brothers and sisters deserve respect, too, no matter how much they drive you crazy. Let your sister watch the channel she wants to watch, or let your brother sit in the front seat of the car. Remember to take turns!

There are many stories, fairy tales, and poems that help us learn to be kind and respectful. Some good examples are: *Frog and Toad Together* and *The House at Pooh Corner*, or *The Gift of the Magi*. Or you can watch a good video with your family—like *Heidi*, *Charlotte's Web*, or *The Hobbit*.

A Way to Love

When we show respect, we take the time to look carefully, to pay attention. We see that there is more to a person than just what shows on the outside. We understand that, on the inside, we are all children of God and we all deserve respect.

Respect is really another word for love. When you respect others, you accept them just as they are—along with their feelings, tastes, and rights. When someone respects you, it lets you know you are loved just for being you.

You can bring more love into the world. Dare to care, share, and be fair...RESPECT!

Ted O'Neal is the father of three children, and author of the Elf-help book *Garden Therapy*. He lives in southern Indiana and has written for various family publications. **Jenny O'Neal**, the respectful and much-respected daughter of Ted O'Neal, is a student majoring in child psychology at Indiana University.

R. W. Alley is the illustrator for the popular Abbey Press adult series of Elf-help books, as well as an illustrator and writer of children's books. He lives in Barrington, Rhode Island, with his wife, daughter, and son. See a wide variety of his works at: www.rwalley.com.